J 597.9638 Whi

W9-BLT-102

Fangs
DIAMONDBACK
RATTLERS

America's Most Venomous Snakes!

by Nancy White

Consultant: Raoul Bain, Biodiversity Specialist, Herpetology
Center for Biodiversity and Conservation
American Museum of Natural History
New York, New York

BEARPORT
PUBLISHING

New York, New York

Credits

Cover and Title Page, © Rick and Nora Bowers/Alamy; TOC, © John Bell/Shutterstock; 4-5, © Joel Sartore/National Geographic/Getty Images; 6, © Robin Brandt; 7, © John R. MacGregor/africa-photo/Peter Arnold Inc.; 8, © blickwinkel/Alamy; 9, © Joe McDonald/Animals Animals Enterprises; 10-11, © Dave Welling; 12, © Jack Goldfarb; 13, © Joe McDonald/Visuals Unlimited/Getty Images; 14, © John Bell/Shutterstock; 15, © John Cancalosi/age fotostock/Photolibrary; 16, © Frank Lundburg; 17, © Morgan Ball/Chuck Place Photography; 18, © Matt Meadows/Peter Arnold Inc.; 19, © Wayne Lynch/DRK Photo; 20, © Zigmund Leszczynski/Animals Animals Enterprises; 21, © Paul & Joyce Berquist/Animals Animals Enterprises; 22, © Zoltan Takacs/Bruce Coleman; 23A, © Barry Soames/Alamy; 23B, © Snowleopard1/Shutterstock; 23C, © JH Pete Carmichael/Riser/Getty Images; 23D, © Joe McDonald/Animals Animals Enterprises; 23E, © Matt Meadows/Peter Arnold Inc.; 23F, © Maria Dryfhout/Shutterstock; 23G, © Snowleopard1/Shutterstock; 23H, © Susan Flashman/Shuttterstock; 23I, © Wayne Lynch/DRK Photo; 23B, © John Bell/Shutterstock.

Publisher: Kenn Goin
Senior Editor: Lisa Wiseman
Creative Director: Spencer Brinker
Photo Researcher: Mike Fergenson
Design: Dawn Beard Creative

Library of Congress Cataloging-in-Publication Data

White, Nancy, 1942–
   Diamondback rattlers : America's most venomous snakes! / by Nancy White.
      p. cm. — (Fangs)
   Includes bibliographical references and index.
   ISBN-13: 978-1-59716-765-9 (library binding)
   ISBN-10: 1-59716-765-7 (library binding)
   1. Eastern diamondback rattlesnake—Juvenile literature. 2. Western diamondback rattlesnake—Juvenile literature. I. Title.

QL666.069W476 2009
597.96'38—dc22

2008045417

For more information, write to Bearport Publishing Company, Inc., 101 Fifth Avenue, Suite 6R, New York, New York 10003. Printed in the United States of America.

10 9 8 7 6 5 4 3 2 1

Contents

A Painful Discovery

At first, the only sounds the campers heard in the dark forest were their own voices as they searched for firewood. Suddenly, they heard a low rattling sound. The campers looked around nervously. Then they saw it—a diamondback rattler, America's most **venomous** snake! With its head raised off the ground and its mouth open wide, the snake hissed loudly and struck—biting one of them on the hand.

Instantly, the pain was terrible. The camper's hand swelled as the venom began to destroy the flesh. Without medicine, he might die. Even with medicine, he could lose a few fingers—or his entire hand!

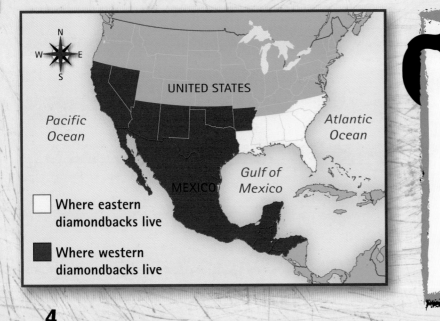

UNITED STATES

Pacific
Ocean

Atlantic
Ocean

Gulf of
Mexico

MEXICO

☐ Where eastern
diamondbacks live

■ Where western
diamondbacks live

There are many types of rattlesnakes, but only two of them are diamondbacks. The eastern diamondback lives along the southeast coast of the United States, while the western diamondback lives in the southwestern part of the country as well as in Mexico.

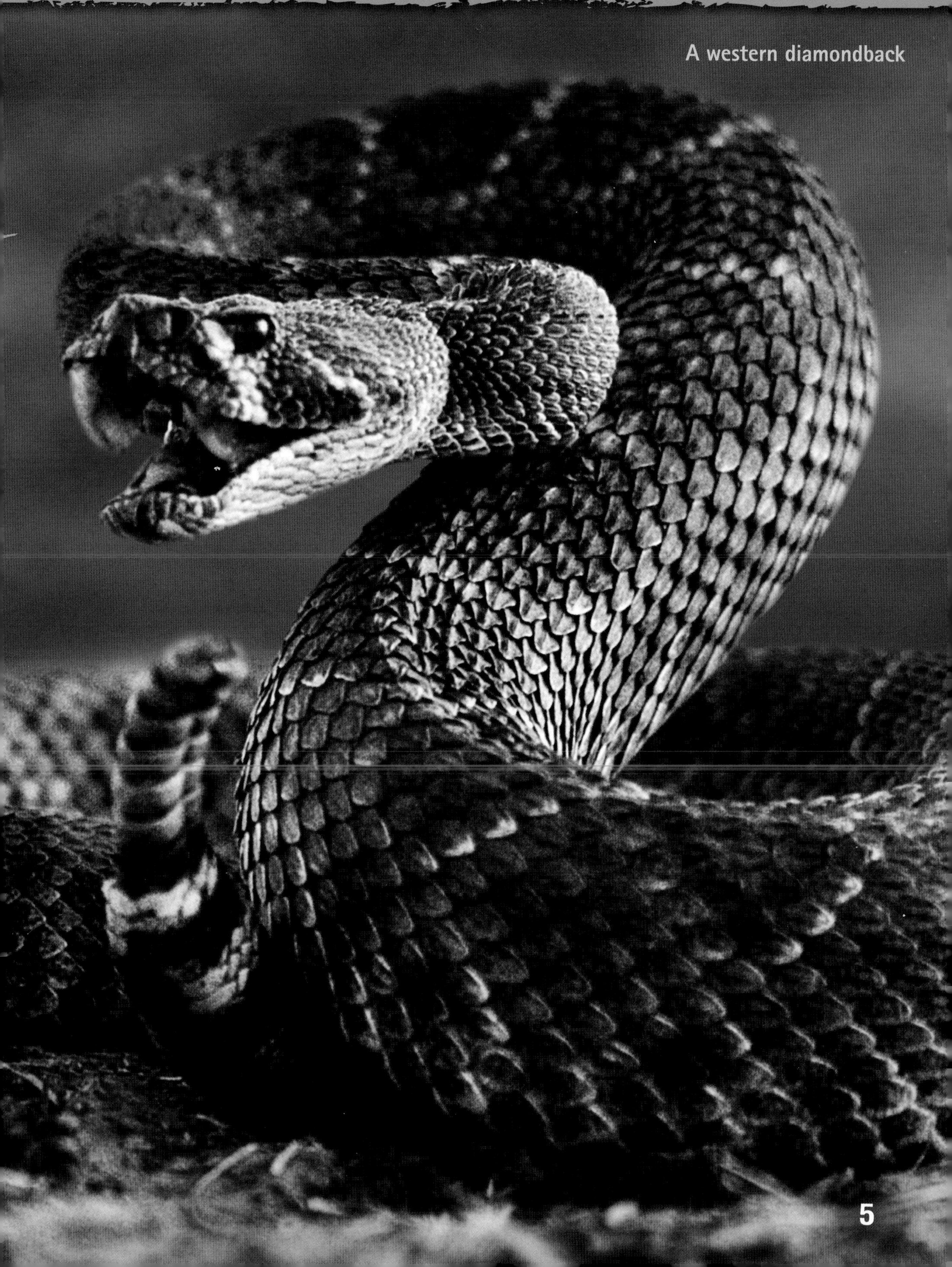

A western diamondback

Comparing Killers

Though they're both rattlers, the two types of diamondbacks don't look exactly alike. Eastern diamondbacks are darker colored and tend to be bigger than their western cousins. The largest ones are eight feet (2.4 m) long—about the length of a Ping-Pong table. The largest western diamondbacks are less than seven feet (2.1 m) long.

The two diamondbacks do have several features in common, however. Both have thick bodies, narrow necks, and large triangle-shaped heads. On their backs, they each have dark-colored diamond shapes, outlined in white or yellow. Their tails have black and white stripes. These colors and patterns protect the snakes by camouflaging them, or helping them blend in with their surroundings.

Western diamondbacks are lighter in color than eastern diamondbacks.

eastern diamondback rattler

Eastern diamondbacks are considered to be the largest and heaviest venomous snakes in North and South America. They can weigh up to 10 pounds (4.5 kg).

The Sound of Death

Both eastern and western diamondbacks have hard rings, or rattles, around the ends of their tails. When these snakes are angry or frightened, they usually shake their tails so that the rings hit one another, making a rattling sound.

A diamondback gets a new rattle each time it **sheds** its skin. How? First, the snake makes a tear in its old skin by rubbing its head and neck against a rock or a log. Then the snake wiggles forward, peeling off the skin from head to tail. In the same way that a sock might come off a foot, the skin comes off inside out, showing the brand-new skin underneath. A ring of old skin, however, sticks to the end of the tail. That ring becomes a new rattle.

rattles

old skin

new skin

When a diamondback starts rattling, the sound is like bones hitting one another. If the snake is really angry or scared, it shakes its tail faster, and the sound turns into a loud buzz. Anyone who knows that sound fears it. It means the killer is about to strike!

Self-Defense

Why are rattles so important? They can save a diamondback's life! Even though the snakes' colors help them blend into their environments, hawks, coyotes, foxes, other snakes, and humans may still be able to spot them. Rattling can scare these enemies away.

When rattling doesn't frighten away an enemy, the diamondback has other ways of defending itself. It can **coil** its lower body, raise its upper body, and then open its mouth wide and hiss loudly. If that doesn't scare off the enemy, the snake may then strike, bite, and try to kill.

One of the eastern diamondback's enemies is the king snake. It's not venomous itself and it can't be killed by rattlesnake venom. The king snake kills by wrapping itself around the diamondback and squeezing it to death. The western diamondback has a different enemy—the roadrunner. This small bird hops around so quickly that it can avoid the rattler's strikes before it kills the snake with its strong, sharp beak.

A diamondback rattlesnake in a defensive position

A Hidden Hunter

Western diamondbacks hunt mainly at night, while eastern diamondbacks hunt mostly around dusk or dawn—when the sun is setting or rising. Since the snakes are hidden by the dark, their **victims** often don't see them until it's too late.

A diamondback usually hides behind rocks or under leaves when it's getting ready to attack. When an unlucky animal comes along, the snake opens its jaws wide, lunges forward, and stabs its victim with its **fangs**, injecting a large dose of deadly venom. Then it lets go and pulls back. All this happens in less than one second!

▲ A diamondback waiting to attack

Smaller diamondbacks hunt mice, lizards, frogs, and little birds. Larger ones kill and eat rats, gophers, rabbits, and squirrels.

A diamondback in mid-strike

13

A Quick Death

Once the diamondback lets go of its prey, the victim tries to escape. However, it won't live long enough to get very far. In one to two minutes, the snake's powerful venom stops the victim's heart and lungs from working.

Once the **prey** stops moving, the killer stretches its jaws wide. It uses its fangs to pull the lifeless victim's head into its mouth and then it swallows the rest of the animal. After that, the snake rests as it digests its meal. A week might go by before the diamondback has to eat again.

fangs

wide jaw

A diamondback can
swallow an animal as
big as a rabbit. How? The snake
is able to disconnect its jaw
bones, which allows its mouth
to open extra-wide.

A Strike in the Dark

Diamondbacks rely on their senses when hunting. The pupils in their eyes open very wide to let in every bit of light. This allows them to see better in the dark than most other animals. They smell prey both with their nostrils and their forked tongues, which they flick in and out to bring scents from the air into their mouths.

In addition to using their eyes, nostrils, and tongues, diamondbacks still have another way of finding prey. Diamondbacks belong to a group of snakes called pit vipers. These animals depend on two small round openings on the sides of their faces, called pits, to sense the heat that other animals give off. The pits help the snakes pinpoint exactly where prey is located. They allow these killers to strike accurately even on the darkest nights.

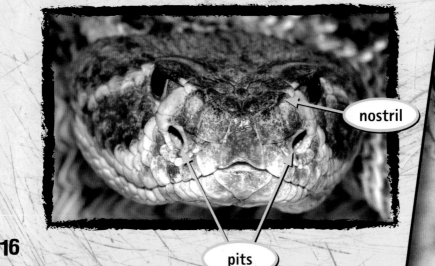

nostril

pits

More than 270 different types of snakes are pit vipers.

eye

forked tongue

pit

Sleeping Killers

Diamondbacks can hunt when it's dark, but not when it's cold! In cold weather, they can't move, which means they can't look for food. Then how do they keep from starving in winter? They **hibernate**.

When it gets cold, diamondbacks find a **den**, usually in a **burrow**. Inside, as many as 500 snakes coil together in a huge ball! The snakes stay inside until the temperature outside gets warmer. Then they leave the den, warm up their bodies in the sun, and go hunting. After all, they're pretty hungry after months of not eating.

A diamondback in the entranceway to its den

In places where the winters are long and cold, diamondbacks may hibernate for as many as nine months. In places with shorter winters, they might stay in their dens for only two months.

Baby's First Rattle

In late summer, before hibernating, a female diamondback gives birth to 8 to 14 live babies. The little rattlers are only 9 to 14 inches (23 to 36 cm) long, but they are born with sharp fangs and deadly venom. They can kill their first lizard or mouse about two weeks after birth.

Although it's deadly, a newborn diamondback has no rattles—just a knob at the end of its tail. When the baby snake sheds for the first time, a little ring of skin gets stuck on that knob. After the second shedding, another ring of skin gets stuck. Then the baby snake can make one of the most feared sounds on earth—the bone-chilling rattle of a master killer!

adult diamondback rattler

newborn diamondback rattlers

A baby diamondback
rattlesnake

While baby diamondback rattlers
are small, they can be even
more dangerous to humans than adult
snakes. The reason for this is that they
have less control over the amount of
venom they inject when they bite.

Fang Facts

- About ten people in the United States die each year from venomous rattlesnake bites, mostly from diamondbacks.

- Like all venomous snakes, a diamondback rattler has two fangs attached to its upper jaw. These sharp fangs, which can be more than one inch (2.5 cm) long, can easily slice into an animal's skin and squirt deadly venom deep into the wound.

fang

- A diamondback keeps its fangs folded up against the roof of its mouth. Its fangs are so long that if they didn't fold back, the snake wouldn't be able to close its mouth!

- When a diamondback is about to strike, its fangs spring forward and snap into place.

- Diamondback rattlers often lose fangs. Each time a fang comes out, however, a new one is ready to take its place.

- A diamondback's venom is so strong that dried venom can keep its strength for 50 years!

- Touching a rattlesnake that has been recently killed is dangerous. A rattlesnake can even strike and inject venom shortly after it has died!

Glossary

burrow
(BUR-oh) a hole or tunnel in the ground used by an animal to live in

prey
(PRAY) animals that are hunted and eaten by other animals

coil
(KOIL) to wind around and around in loops

sheds
(SHEDZ) loses a layer of skin

den
(DEN) an enclosed place where a wild animal can stay hidden

venomous
(VEN-uhm-uhss) full of poison

fangs
(FANGZ) long pointy teeth

victims
(VIK-tuhmz) animals that are attacked or killed by other animals

hibernate
(HYE-bur-nate) to go into a sleeplike state during periods of cold weather

Index

Read More

Arnosky, Jim. *All About Rattlesnakes.* New York: Scholastic (1997).

Feldman, Heather. *Diamondbacks.* New York: PowerKids Press (2004).

Gerholdt, James E. *Diamondback Rattlesnakes.* Edina, MN: ABDO (1996).

Learn More Online

To learn more about diamondback rattlers, visit
www.bearportpublishing.com/Fangs

About the Author

Nancy White has written many science and nature books for children. She lives with her husband and her cat in New York's Hudson River Valley.